U.S. Fish & Wildlife Service

SHOREBIRDS—MIGRATORY SUPER HEROES!

A Student Activity Guide

Dear Educator,

Welcome to the fascinating world of shorebirds! The diversity of physical and behavioral adaptations of shorebirds, plus the shear magnitude of their global migration, make them a captivating topic for students. This activity guide can be used by students alone or along with the Shorebird Sister Schools curriculum. The activities vary in difficulty and are designed to meet various learning levels from 2nd through 6th grades. Please send your comments and questions to the Shorebird Sister Schools Program coordinator at sssp@fws.gov or by calling 304/876 7783.

National Wildlife Refuges

The U.S. Fish and Wildlife Service manages national wildlife refuges, the world's largest and most diverse collection of lands set aside specifically for wildlife. Many refuges provide important habitat for migrating and nesting shorebirds.

March 14, 2003 marked the 100th anniversary of the National Wildlife Refuge System. Pelican Island, Florida, was the first national wildlife refuge established by President Theodore Roosevelt in 1903. Since then, more than 500 refuges have been designated. They include nearly 100 million acres across the United States and its territories. Looking at this map, is there a refuge in your state? To learn more go to http://refuges.fws.gov.

Division of Migratory Bird Management

Working with partners, the U.S. Fish and Wildlife Service is responsible for providing global leadership in the conservation and management of migratory birds for present and future generations. For more information go to http://migratorybirds.fws.gov. For more information on shorebird conservation go to http://shorebirdplan.fws.gov.

Western Hemisphere Shorebird Reserve Network (WHSRN)

Many National Wildlife Refuges are also important shorebird sites. These sites are part of a network specifically established for shorebirds, called the Western Hemisphere Shorebird Reserve Network (WHSRN). WHSRN gives refuges international recognition for providing habitat for shorebirds. For more information go to http://www.manomet.org/WHSRN

● *Indicates a Refuge*

ANIMAL SUPER HEROES

Superbirds!
- Able to cross oceans in a single bound!

- Weighing no more than a few ounces (several quarters).

- Not quite as fast as a speeding bullet but pretty darn fast!

No, we are not talking about Superman. We are talking about shorebirds... the rugged super heroes of the animal kingdom that can be found sticking their beaks in the mud, chasing down a meal in the many small and large wetlands across North America.

World Travelers!
So, you don't think that these little puffs of feathers running around in the mud are worthy of super hero status? Well, think again! Today they may be running around the edges of a pond near your town, but within the last few weekends, those little balls of fluff may have been sticking their beaks in the mud of some faraway countries such as Argentina, Brazil, Suriname, Venezuela, and Mexico.

Super Bird Food!
OK, sticking your beak in the mud, and eating grubby little mud-sucking creatures isn't a typical super hero activity. But just like Popeye and his spinach, those unappetizing little creatures that shorebirds eat give them the energy to do some pretty spectacular things. Still not convinced? Well, read on and do the activities in this guide to learn more. Then decide for yourself if you think that they qualify as super heroes of the animal kingdom.

WHO ARE THESE SUPER HEROES?

There are 49 different species of shorebirds found in North America. What they mainly have in common are their long beaks, legs, toes, long pointy wings, and the ability to build up and store fat. The long beaks, legs, and toes are perfect for wading around in search of food in the mud and shallow water of the wetlands and coastal beaches where they live.

Some shorebirds, like the Killdeer, may spend their summers in your neighborhood or on your school grounds feeding and nesting. Killdeers move to the southern United States, Mexico, or Central America in the winter to find food. Others, like the Hudsonian Godwit, fly each spring from the very southern tip of South America to the Arctic Circle and back. This round-trip journey is over 20,000 miles!

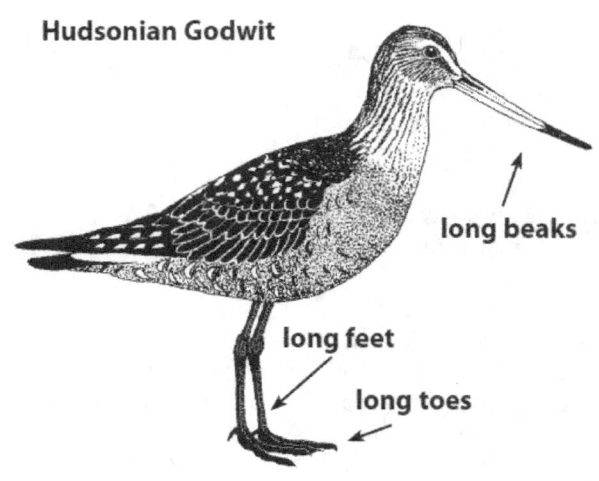

Hudsonian Godwit

long beaks

long feet

long toes

Black-bellied Plover

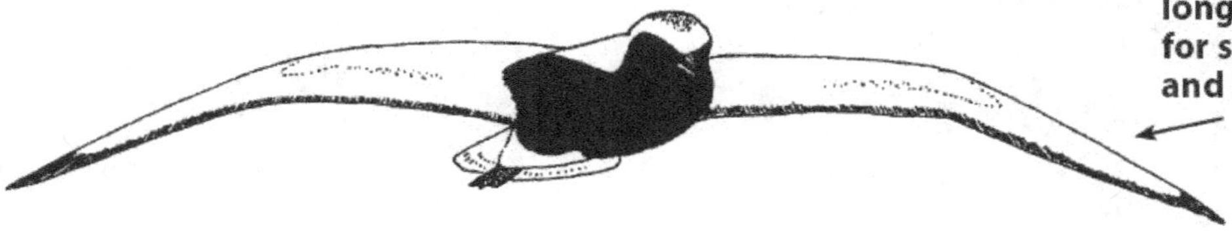

long narrow wings for speed, agility, and long flights

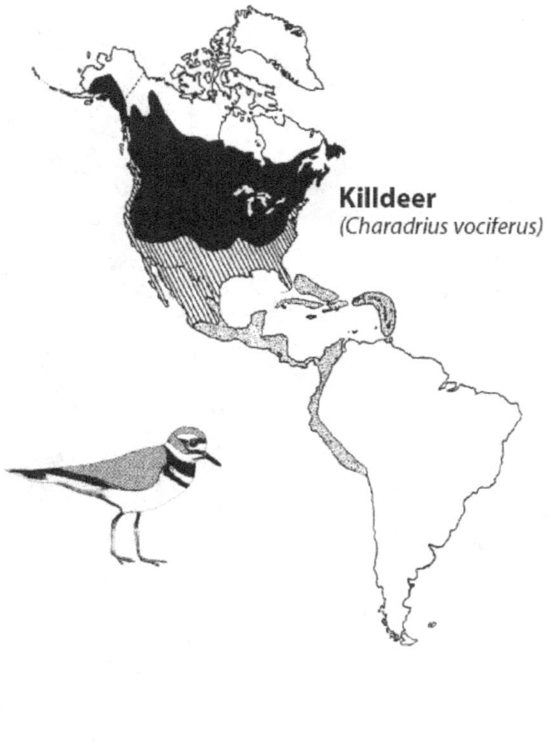

Killdeer
(*Charadrius vociferus*)

Hudsonian Godwit
(*Limosa haemastica*)

Key

▉ Breeding area

\\\\ Resident year round

░ Wintering area

SHOREBIRDS WORD SEARCH

Read about shorebirds and then find the hidden words in the puzzle. The words to look for are in bold letters. Search for the words across, up, and down and diagonally in all directions.

S	A	N	D	Y	B	E	A	C	H	E	S	I	P	J
E	V	P	E	T	T	M	I	D	O	X	D	J	U	P
T	O	R	G	S	A	R	M	X	L	K	R	S	G	L
A	C	E	A	A	T	E	I	Q	L	I	I	K	X	O
R	E	D	L	R	I	F	G	S	O	L	B	D	G	V
B	T	A	F	D	B	U	R	X	W	L	E	N	J	E
E	S	T	U	N	A	E	A	W	B	D	R	U	S	R
T	L	O	O	U	H	L	T	E	O	E	O	O	X	S
R	L	R	M	T	G	M	E	E	N	E	H	M	D	T
E	Y	S	A	N	D	P	I	P	E	R	S	N	U	A
V	L	E	C	S	D	N	A	L	S	S	A	R	G	L
N	F	S	T	L	I	T	S	W	E	L	R	U	C	F
I	C	H	J	L	A	D	A	P	T	E	D	R	G	D
X	K	R	O	I	V	A	H	E	B	P	Y	F	H	U
F	D	X	N	B	P	C	W	K	M	W	E	N	G	M

Shorebirds are a group of birds **adapted** to live near water. They include **plovers**, **sandpipers**, **curlews**, **avocets**, and **stilts**. **Killdeers** are a type of shorebird too. They use a variety of wetland **habitat** types including rivers and streams, **tundra**, **mudflats**, estuaries, bogs, and **sandy beaches**. Some shorebirds such as killdeers are adapted to live in **grasslands**.

Shorebirds have several adaptations to help them **fly**. They have **hollow bones** which provide a strong but lightweight framework. Their **feathers** are also light and provide them with warmth as well as coloration. Their wings are long and pointed, perfect for long flights. Variations in the shape and size of their **bill**, the length of their legs, and their color can help you tell the different species apart. Their **behavior** also varies from species to species. They usually **nest** on the ground and their eggs are **camouflaged** to help them hide from **predators**. Most shorebirds feed on **invertebrates** found in **wetlands**.

Shorebirds may **migrate** great distances between their breeding and wintering areas. They may need to stop and **refuel** and rest along the way.

BUILD A SHOREBIRD, BUILD MAYA!

Add the correct beak, legs, feet and wings to complete the shorebird.

What *beak* would best help a shorebird probe in the mud for food?

Which *legs* would best suit a shorebird for its wetland habitat?

Which *feet* would best suit a shorebird for walking in its wetland habitat?

What type of *wings* help the shorebird fly long distance and escape quickly from predators?

Answers: page 32

WILSON PHALAROPE CONNECT THE DOTS

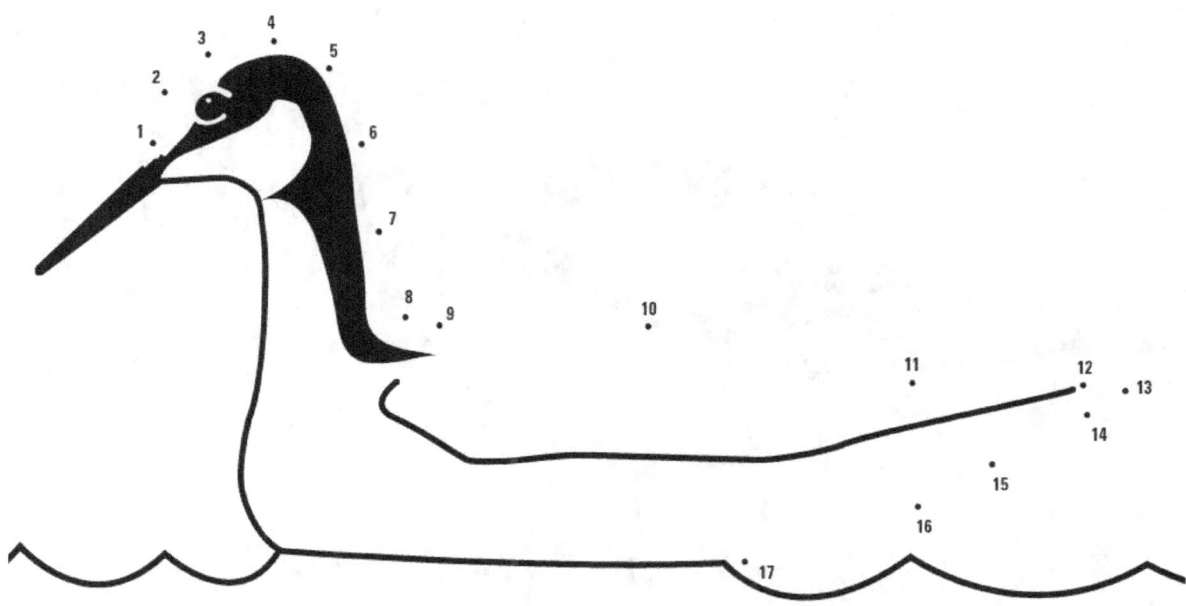

I swim in the water a lot, spinning in circles to help my food come to the surface where I can reach it with my long pointed bill. I nest in the western United States and central Canada. I spend my winters in South America. During migration, I flock with others in large numbers at the Great Salt Lake in Utah. Unlike most birds, females are more colorful than males during the breeding season. I am a Wilson's Phalarope. **Find a bird field guide and color me.**

AMERICAN AVOCET CONNECT THE DOTS

In the spring my head, neck, and chest are a bright orange color. My wings are black and white. Like most shorebirds I nest on the ground. My eggs are speckled and this camouflage helps me hide them from predators. I swish my curved bill in the water and use it to find food. In the winter I live in Mexico, Central America, and along the Gulf Coast of the United States. In the spring, I migrate to breed in western United States and southern Canada. I am an American Avocet. **Find a bird field guide and color me**.

KILLDEER CONNECT THE DOTS

I am a shorebird even though I am often not found next to water. You have probably seen me near a road or in a pasture. If predators get too close to my eggs, I will try to distract them and lead them away by pretending to have a broken wing. My two dark chest bands help identify me as a Killdeer. Also, I call my name when I fly, 'kill-deer, kill-deer.'

WHAT CAN I EAT WITH THIS BEAK?

Activity Background: In a wetland or on a beach food is everywhere. Even though you cannot easily see it—shorebirds can! Each shorebird species has a uniquely adapted beak to find its food.

Activity Instructions: Below is a picture of a beach with food buried in the soil. Your task is to read the clues for each of the shorebird species and choose which food item in the picture you think the bird is best adapted to eat.

Sanderling: I nab insects on the surface of the sand and mud with my beak.

Whimbrel: I am a Whimbrel. I use my down–curved bill to probe **very** deeply into the mud for my food.

Western Sandpiper: Some people think my beak looks like tweezers when I eat. I probe the mud near the surface.

Long–billed Dowitcher: The clue is in my name! I probe deeply in the mud for food.

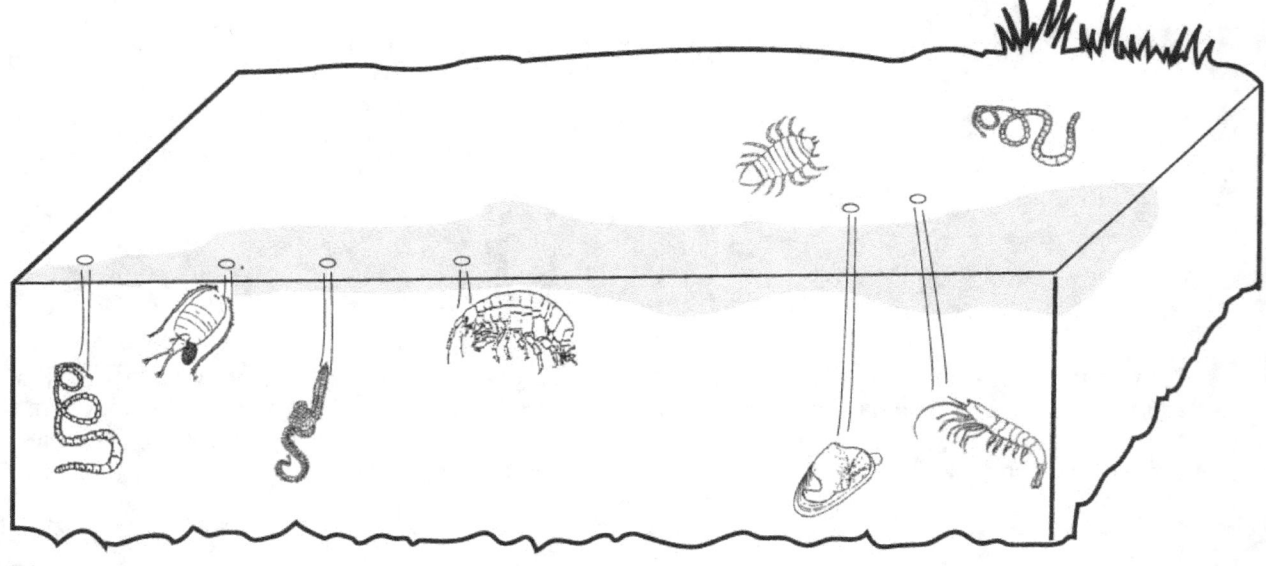

Answers: page 32

OLYMPIC FLYERS!

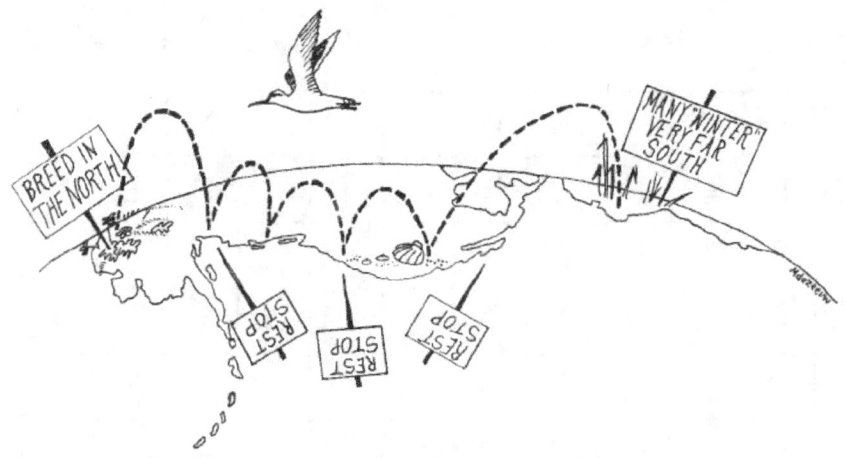

Great concentrations of shorebirds fly thousands of miles every spring and fall to and from their breeding grounds. During their long journey they stop at a variety of habitats including wetlands, grasslands, and sandy beaches to rest and feed.

Like many birds, shorebirds move to find better food supplies as the seasons change. This movement is called migration. Many shorebirds migrate to South America during the winter to avoid the cold. Countries south of the equator have the opposite seasons we do. When it is winter here, it is summer in Argentina. When the days become colder in South America, they are just beginning to get warmer in North America. Shorebirds fly north to take advantage of the insect-rich North American summer.

SHOREBIRD MIGRATION WORD SEARCH

Read about shorebirds and then find the hidden words in the puzzle. The words to look for are in bold letters. Search for the words across, up, and down and diagonally in all directions.

I	G	S	E	A	S	O	N	B	A	N	D	I	N	G
F	N	E	U	H	Q	N	O	I	T	U	L	L	O	P
A	I	V	T	H	B	W	M	N	U	R	E	S	T	B
D	T	R	E	B	I	O	L	O	G	I	S	T	R	O
T	S	E	R	R	C	W	B	C	N	T	T	A	E	U
C	E	S	R	W	T	T	E	U	O	K	I	T	V	R
O	N	E	I	F	E	E	D	L	L	D	M	I	O	M
J	R	R	T	W	D	C	B	A	H	U	A	B	P	J
F	E	T	O	C	C	F	U	R	E	H	T	A	O	A
E	T	A	R	G	I	M	H	S	A	Y	E	H	T	Y
H	N	F	Y	R	P	R	E	D	A	T	O	R	S	G
S	I	S	D	J	L	L	B	W	I	T	E	I	Q	T
O	W	H	H	K	C	T	Y	A	J	C	T	S	K	W
N	S	P	T	A	Q	L	P	T	Y	W	O	A	S	B
J	C	A	X	Y	F	M	I	S	T	N	E	T	S	M

Shorebirds **migrate** between their wintering and breeding grounds each year. Many follow a path called a **flyway**. Some birds may travel a **long** distance each **season**. Birds that nest in the Arctic may spend the **winter** in South America. Many **feed** on **invertebrates** to build up their **fat reserves** and **rest** at **stopover** sites along the way. Along the way, shorebirds may face many potential threats. Loss of **habitat**, **pollution**, and **predators**, such as falcons and owls, can all be hazardous to migrating, wintering, and **nesting** shorebirds. These are all limiting factors that affect how many shorebirds there are.

A **biologist** studying migrating shorebirds may catch them and put a metal ring around their leg. They use fine nets called **mist nets,** which are similar to hair nets, to catch the shorebirds. By **banding** the birds, biologists can learn where an individual bird goes when it leaves an area, how long it may live, and more about its behavior.

Binoculars are helpful to view birds from a distance. Next time you are watching birds, see if you can **estimate** how many birds are in a flock or tell if they are defending a feeding **territory** from each other.

Answers: page 32

SHOREBIRD MIGRATION CROSSWORD PUZZLE — TEST WHAT YOU HAVE LEARNED!

Across

5. Necessary to gain for migration

7. Educated guess of numbers

8. Limits shorebird numbers

9. What migrating birds are looking for

10. Seasonal movement between two spots

Down

1. Scientist who studies wildlife

2. Large groups found at migratory stopovers

3. Way of marking birds

4. Migratory routes

6. Dangers

Answers: page 33

MINDFUL OF MIGRATION

If you are visiting a National Wildlife Refuge that is a migration stopover site during spring, you will probably see thousands of shorebirds. But if you are visiting the refuge in the summertime, you might only see a handful. Where have all the shorebirds gone? Many birds have both summer and winter homes. Each year they make the same round–trip flight, or migration, from one home to the other. Why would they make this long and dangerous trip every year? Most North American birds migrate south for the winter to follow warmer weather and abundant food supplies and return north to nest when spring has sprung.

Chincoteague National Wildlife Refuge in Virginia is located on the Atlantic flyway, a common route for migrating birds. More than 320 species of birds use the refuge as a stopover to rest and eat during their long journeys.

Refuge biologists keep track of the bird species using the refuge. This information is used to follow trends or patterns in bird populations and to change the refuge's management practices if necessary.

Activity Instructions: Study the shorebird surveys below. Based on the survey information, graph when those birds are at the refuge and answer the questions.

Questions:
If Dunlins are at the Chincoteague National Wildlife Refuge in fall through spring, where do they go in the summer?

Do you think Piping Plovers breed at the refuge or simply stop to rest during their migration?

Do you think Least Sandpipers breed at Chincoteague or simply stop to rest during their migration?

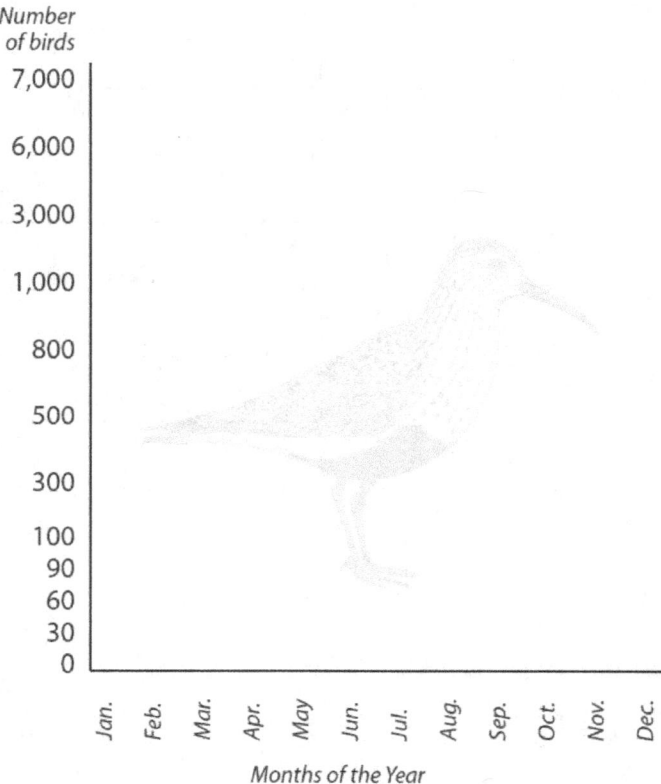

Number of birds

7,000

6,000

3,000

1,000

800

500

300

100
90
60
30
0

Jan. Feb. Mar. Apr. May Jun. Jul. Aug. Sep. Oct. Nov. Dec.

Months of the Year

Chincoteague National Wildlife Refuge – Shorebird Survey

	Jan.	Feb.	Mar.	Apr.	May	Jun.	Jul.	Aug.	Sep.	Oct.	Nov.	Dec.
Dunlin	357	848	526	806	6,663	4	0	0	0	99	2,356	427
Least Sandpiper	0	2	0	58	1,253	0	595	61	70	0	5	0
Piping Plover	0	0	30	60	66	90	90	80	30	0	0	0

SUPER APPETITES & AMAZING FLYERS

So you think that nothing can possibly eat as much as your big brother? Well, shorebirds have an ability to put away food that would put a teenager to shame! To make up for all the weight that they lose during their long flights, they feed nearly continuously on insects, small worms, and other food items. Although they may arrive in their resting areas half-starved, they can nearly double their weight in just a few weeks. Could you do that? To figure out how much you would have to eat, do the sample problem below.

If a hamburger weighs a quarter pound and an 80-pound student has to double his or her weight in 2 weeks. how many hamburgers would he or she have to eat? _____

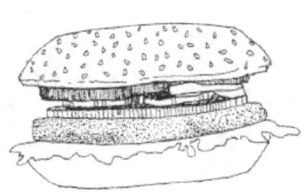

This is of course impossible for humans, but not for our super hero shorebirds. They are able to add enough fat to their bodies to fuel long flights of up to 70 hours without a rest at speeds of up to 60 miles an hour!

The Pacific Golden Plover flies non-stop for 2 to 3 days from Hawaii and other Pacific Islands to Alaska.

How long can you continue to flap your arms?

The tiny Western Sandpiper flies over 250 miles per day between stopover points along the Pacific coast to Alaska. Now that's good mileage!

How far can your family's car go without stopping for gas?

Answers: page 33

WHICH WAY TO THE NESTING GROUNDS?

FINISH

START

Can you help this shorebird find its way to the nesting ground in time to lay eggs and raise young before winter?

Shorebirds take advantage of our insect–rich North American summers to build nests and rear their young. Some find good nesting areas in the grasslands and prairie pothole wetlands of the Great Plains. Others continue even farther north to the Canadian and Alaskan Arctic. On the arctic tundra, the summer only lasts a couple of months. Shorebirds must arrive as soon as it gets warm in order to have time to build their nests, lay their eggs, and raise their young before it gets cold again. By the time winter arrives, both adults and chicks are well on their way south again.

SHOREBIRD HABITAT WORD SEARCH

Read about shorebirds and then find the hidden words in the puzzle. The words to look for are in bold letters. Search for the words across, up, and down and diagonally in all directions.

L	C	Y	C	W	E	T	L	A	N	D	S	S	C	Q
A	O	B	A	I	C	M	H	T	T	G	E	R	I	Y
N	N	Q	M	N	N	Q	C	L	R	T	D	E	T	F
O	S	R	O	T	A	O	A	T	A	I	E	V	C	L
I	E	T	U	E	B	T	E	R	R	I	T	O	R	Y
T	R	V	F	R	R	B	B	P	D	S	S	P	A	W
A	V	T	L	Y	U	E	Y	O	N	N	A	O	Z	A
N	A	R	A	Z	T	O	D	L	U	D	O	T	V	Y
R	T	A	G	R	S	Y	N	L	T	F	C	S	W	S
E	I	S	E	D	I	V	A	U	L	T	P	A	B	P
T	O	V	O	O	D	S	S	T	A	T	I	B	A	H
N	N	O	I	T	A	R	G	I	M	M	O	Z	U	S
I	F	M	J	I	Z	S	R	O	T	A	D	E	R	P
Z	U	G	N	I	T	S	E	N	W	V	O	M	B	L

Habitat provides an animal with the **food**, water, shelter, and space that it needs to live and raise its young. Some examples of shorebird habitat include **wetlands** and grasslands. A **sandy beach** along the **coast** may also be a good area for it to **nest**, spend the **winter,** or feed during **migration**. Since conditions change during the year, shorebirds often migrate long distances to find food and raise their young. During migration they use **flyways**, or routes, to travel from their breeding to their wintering areas and back again. Along flyways they may use **stopover** sites where they rest and feed on **invertebrates**. Many species fly from South America to the Alaskan and Canadian **Arctic** to nest on the treeless, insect–rich **tundra** wetland. Others nest in grasslands along the coasts in the United States and Canada.

Once on their breeding grounds, they quickly set up nesting **territory**. They nest on the ground and depend on their **camouflage** to protect them from **predators**. Most shorebirds nest on the ground in scrapes, shallow depressions, that may be lined with vegetation or small rock chips. Their eggs, usually three or four, are camouflaged to help them hide from predators. One or both parents will incubate the eggs until they hatch. The young leave the nest and begin feeding on bugs right away. The young birds stay with an adult until they fledge, when they grow their flight feathers and learn to fly.

Shorebirds face many different threats such as loss of habitat, **pollution**, and **disturbance** by people. Because they cross boundaries of so many countries, it is important to have **international** cooperation for shorebird **conservation**.

Answers: page 33

SHOREBIRD BREEDING CROSSWORD PUZZLE - TEST YOUR KNOWLEDGE

Across

2. How they got there

5. Where many shorebirds nest

6. Egg and chick defense

7. Make the nest here

8. Food for baby birds

Down

1. Foxes, raptors, and snakes to a shorebird

3. Sitting on eggs to keep them warm

4. When young begin to fly

5. Area a shorebird protects, usually around its nest or feeding area

Answers: page 33

WETLAND STEW FOOD CHAIN GAME

Grasses are the most common plants in many wetlands. These grasses are the building blocks of the wetland food web, providing lots of food for marsh critters. However, most marsh animals, such as some insects and crabs, cannot digest the tough plant material. When the grass dies, bacteria break down the dead leaves and stems through a process known as decomposition. The leftover decomposed matter is then available to other animals in a form they can eat. This decomposed vegetation, along with tiny bits of animal remains, is called detritus. Crabs, fish, mussels, clams, and many other animals feed on detritus. In turn they eventually become food for other animals. Nothing is wasted and everything is dependent upon one another.

Shorebirds are an important part of this food chain. Their waste, or poop, provides important food and nutrients for the bacteria in the wetland.

Activity Instructions: Begin with the detritus and connect each plant or animal to what eats it. More than one animal can feed on the same thing.

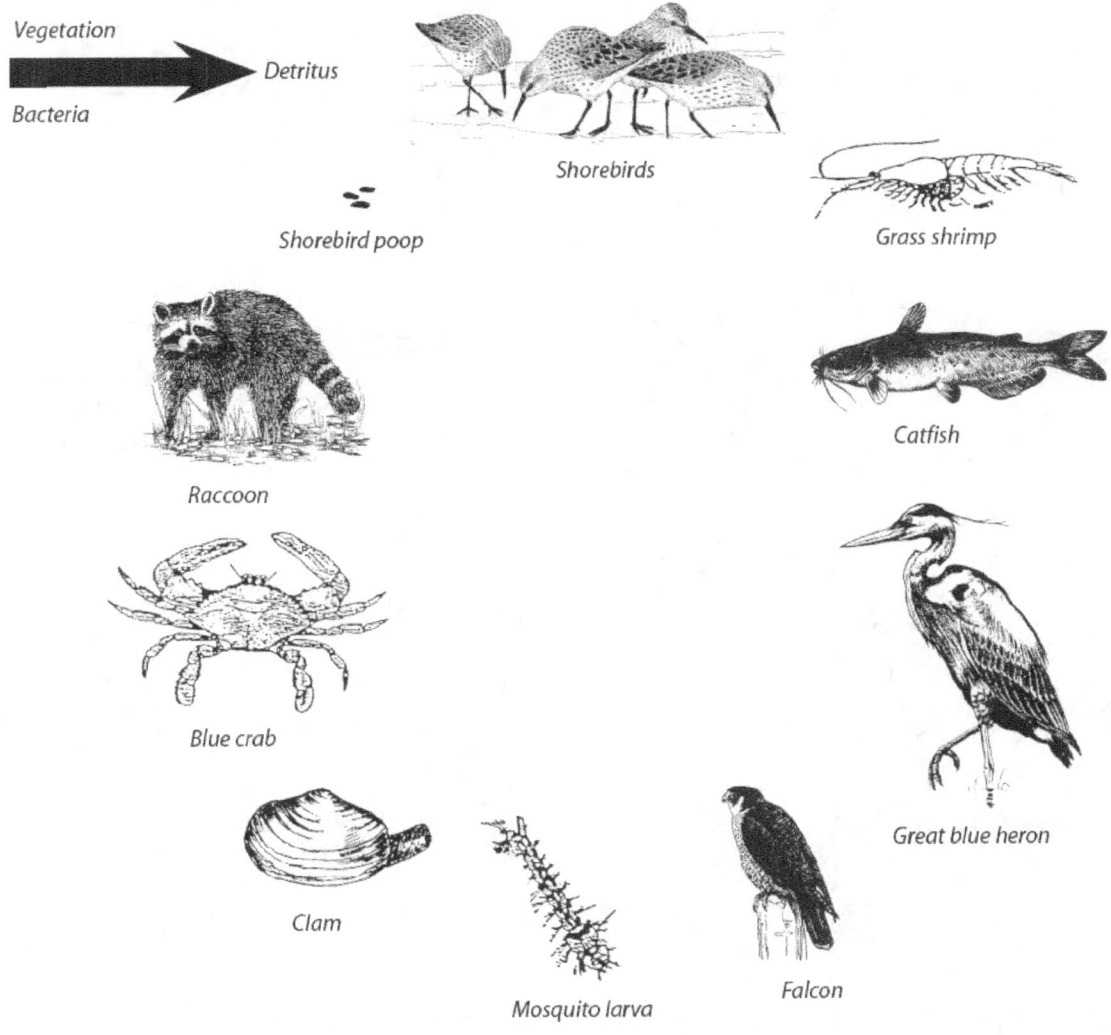

Vegetation
Bacteria → Detritus

Shorebirds

Shorebird poop

Grass shrimp

Raccoon

Catfish

Blue crab

Great blue heron

Clam

Mosquito larva

Falcon

WETLAND METAPHORS

What is a home, a sponge, and a strainer all at the same time?

Metaphors are a way to compare unrelated things, such as "Wes is a barrel of laughs." Below are pictures of items seemingly unrelated to wetlands. Can you figure out how these items compare to a wetland? In other words, think about what each item does. Then compare that item's function to how a wetland might function in that same way. Good luck!

Sponge

_____

Cradle

_____

Pillow

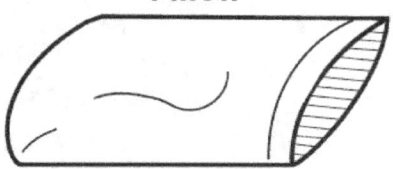

_____

Strainer

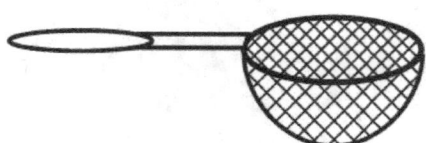

_____

Egg beater

_____

Flower

beautiful places

_____

Can of soup

_____

Answers: page 34

IT'S A TOUGH LIFE FOR A SUPER HERO SHOREBIRD

Shorebirds face many challenges to survive such as loss of habitat, predators, pollution, disturbance by people and pets, disease, and harsh weather. But by far their biggest challenge is the loss of habitat.
Activity Instructions: Below are a number of threats to shorebird survival. Your job is to put each threat in the correct category.

Shorebird Threat Categories	Threats
Predators	fox
	cat
	hurricane
	drought
	flood
Natural Events	raccoon
	parking lot
	disease
	gull
	oil spill
Human Related	trash
	polluted water
	buildings
	filling in wetland
	overgrazing

Which category has the most threats listed under it?

Which threats can we not control?

Can you come up with a solution for one of the human related threats?

Answers: page 34

COLORING PAGE

SHOREBIRD SISTER SCHOOLS – GET CREATIVE!!!

Use your talent to help conserve our migratory super heroes.

How?
Assemble a sandpiper sculpture… Design a dunlin diorama… Photograph a phalarope foraging… Write a ruff rap… Pen a piping plover poem… It's up to you.

Send the Shorebird Sister Schools Program *sssp@fws.gov* an electronic version of your best creative product.

Send all images as a JPG no larger than 1MB in file size and all written works in an MS Word-compatible format.

All submissions must be accompanied by a release form that includes the following statements: "I grant permission to the U.S. Fish & Wildlife Service Shorebird Sister Schools Program to post my photo/essay/poem/etc. on the *http://sssp.fws.gov* site and use it in their publications." "I would like my work to be credited as _____."

DAYS OF OUR LIVES GAME
NESTS AND TALLY SHEET

What You Need: Like on TV soap operas, shorebirds face many perils during their lives. Play the game with three or four of your friends to learn more about shorebird survival. You will need **a die**, a **game piece**, an **egg tally** and **nest sheet** for each player (provided below), and about **forty dry beans** that represent eggs.

How to Play: 1. Start with your game pieces at the wintering grounds. **2.** Taking turns, roll the die and migrate north the number of spaces on the die. If you land on a space with instructions, follow them. **3.** While migrating, keep track of how many eggs you lose or gain on your egg tally sheet. This shows how healthy or sick a bird is and how its health can effect the number of eggs it can lay. **4.** Once you reach the breeding grounds you get 4 eggs (beans) to place in your nest. Subtract or add eggs to your nest depending on the tally from your egg tally sheet. **5.** Then continue rolling the die and following what the spaces tell you. The eggs become young shorebirds when you continue migration back to the wintering grounds, South. **6.** The winner of the game is the shorebird that has the most young left upon returning to the wintering grounds.

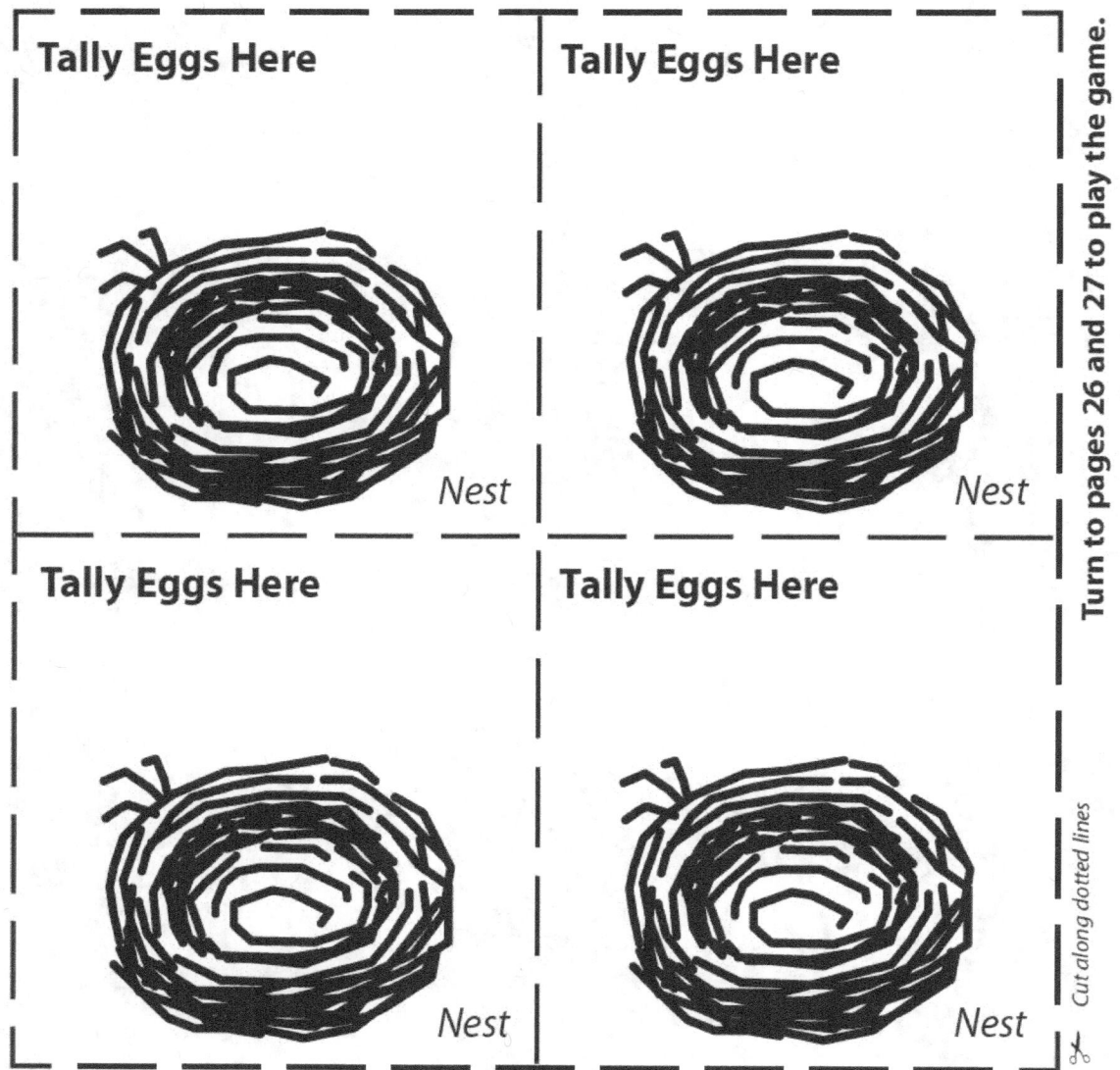

Tally Eggs Here

Nest

Tally Eggs Here

Nest

Tally Eggs Here

Nest

Tally Eggs Here

Nest

Turn to pages 26 and 27 to play the game.

Cut along dotted lines

COLORING PAGE

Use a field guide to learn how to color each bird.

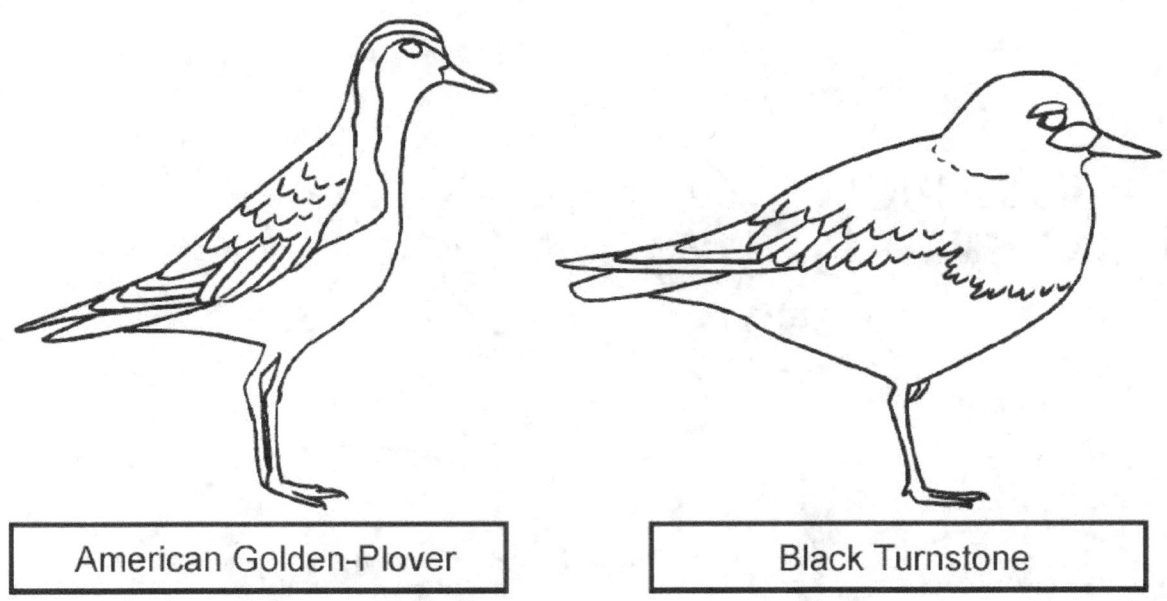

American Golden-Plover

Black Turnstone

Black-Bellied Plover

Ruddy Turnstone

DAYS OF OUR LIVES: SHOREBIRD SOAP OPERAS

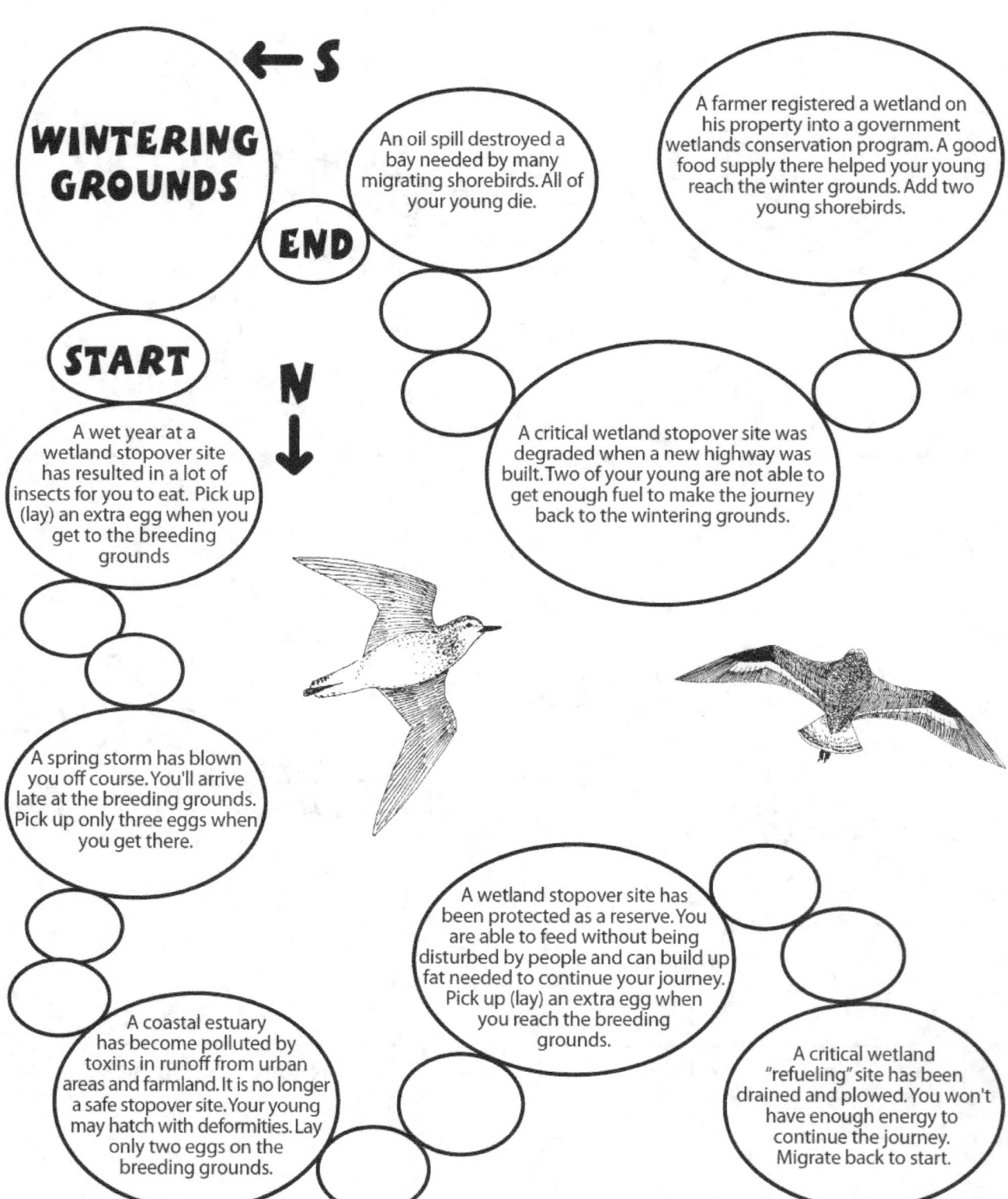

WINTERING GROUNDS

← S

END

An oil spill destroyed a bay needed by many migrating shorebirds. All of your young die.

A farmer registered a wetland on his property into a government wetlands conservation program. A good food supply there helped your young reach the winter grounds. Add two young shorebirds.

START

N

A wet year at a wetland stopover site has resulted in a lot of insects for you to eat. Pick up (lay) an extra egg when you get to the breeding grounds

A critical wetland stopover site was degraded when a new highway was built. Two of your young are not able to get enough fuel to make the journey back to the wintering grounds.

A spring storm has blown you off course. You'll arrive late at the breeding grounds. Pick up only three eggs when you get there.

A coastal estuary has become polluted by toxins in runoff from urban areas and farmland. It is no longer a safe stopover site. Your young may hatch with deformities. Lay only two eggs on the breeding grounds.

A wetland stopover site has been protected as a reserve. You are able to feed without being disturbed by people and can build up fat needed to continue your journey. Pick up (lay) an extra egg when you reach the breeding grounds.

A critical wetland "refueling" site has been drained and plowed. You won't have enough energy to continue the journey. Migrate back to start.

Loose running dogs from a housing development chased you off your nest. You lose two eggs which overheated while you were off the nest.

You managed to scare off a cow that almost trampled your nest. Pick up one more egg.

You defended your eggs from a weasel by pretending to have an injured wing to distract the predator. Pick up two more eggs.

BREEDING GROUNDS

A person riding an ATV through the nesting area accidentally smashed your nest with a tire. You lose all your eggs. Migrate to the end.

A fox discovered your nest and destroyed one of your eggs.

You chose a well camouflaged nest site and your eggs are safe. Add one egg.

Unexpected high water levels flooded your nest. Two eggs are destroyed.

Human access to the nesting beach has been restricted. You are able to double clutch (produce two sets of chicks in a row). Pick up four extra eggs.

EVEN SUPER HEROES NEED OUR HELP

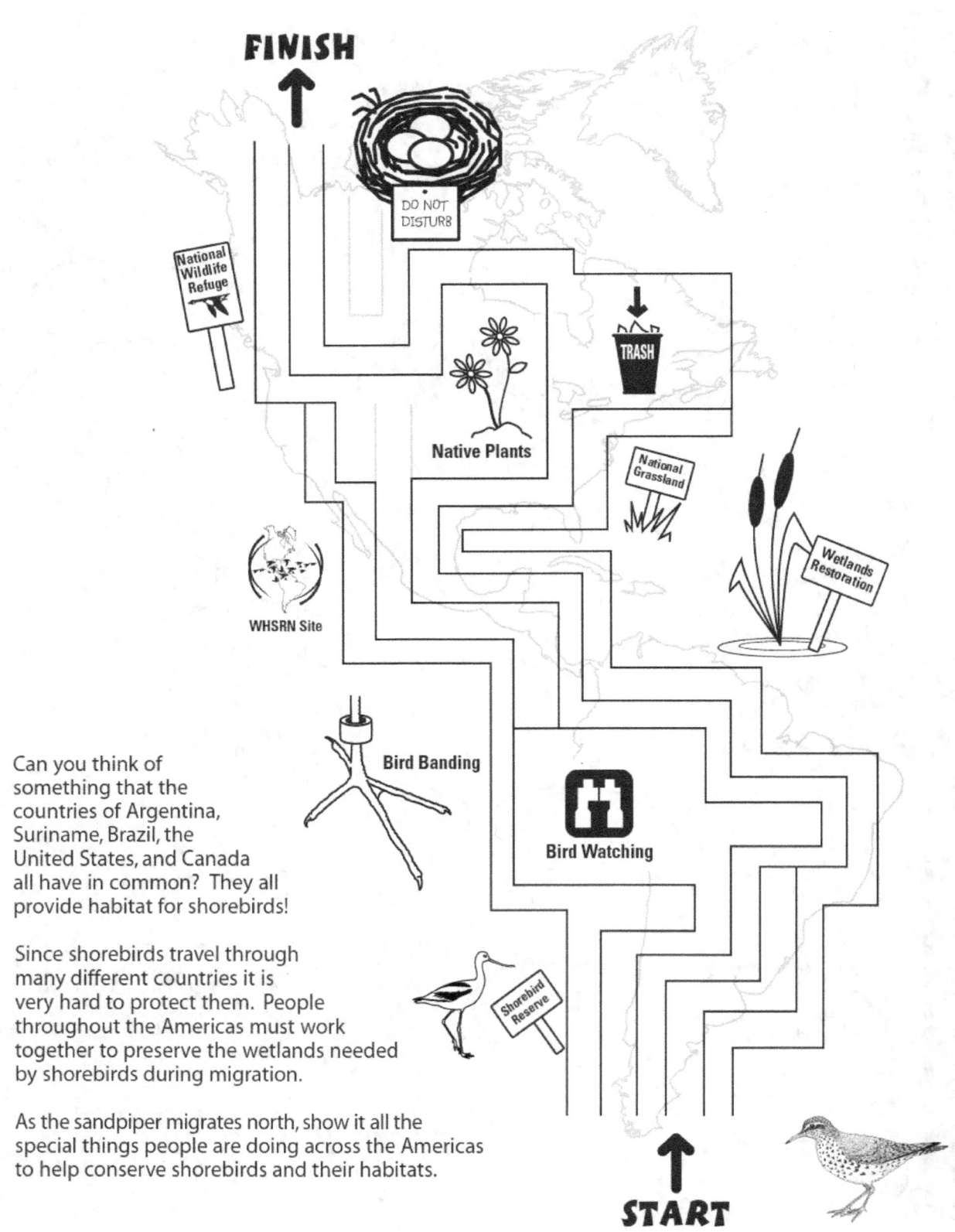

FINISH

DO NOT DISTURB

National Wildlife Refuge

Native Plants

TRASH

National Grassland

Wetlands Restoration

WHSRN Site

Bird Banding

Bird Watching

Shorebird Reserve

START

Can you think of something that the countries of Argentina, Suriname, Brazil, the United States, and Canada all have in common? They all provide habitat for shorebirds!

Since shorebirds travel through many different countries it is very hard to protect them. People throughout the Americas must work together to preserve the wetlands needed by shorebirds during migration.

As the sandpiper migrates north, show it all the special things people are doing across the Americas to help conserve shorebirds and their habitats.

LEARNING ABOUT SHOREBIRDS IS HELPING THEM!

Learning about and becoming aware of shorebirds and their habitat are the first steps in helping to conserve them. Test your knowledge with these puzzles.

Down

2. _____are animal super heroes.

3. Shorebirds have long legs and_____, which are perfect for getting around and feeding in wetlands.

5. A baby bird is called a_____.

6. Shorebirds can nearly double their_____in just a few weeks by eating many small insects and worms.

7. Most shorebirds live near_____. These areas provide them with the food and shelter that they need.

8. The Western_____probes the mud near the surface for food.

Across

1. A prairie_____is a small wetland found in the Great Plains.

4. Many shorebirds lay their eggs and raise their young in the _____, where summers are very short.

8. When it is fall in South America it is_____in North America.

9. Wetlands help prevent_____by holding excess water during heavy rains.

10. Shorebirds stick their beaks in the_____to find insects and worms to eat.

11. People in Argentina speak this language.

12. Many shorebirds_____from South America to North America each year to take advantage of the North American summer to lay their eggs and raise their young.

SHOREBIRD CIRCLE PUZZLE

Directions

The seven sentences at the bottom of the page are clues to the seven corresponding word banks above. Fill in the blank spaces by figuring out the clues. When you have filled in all the blanks, the circled letters will spell the mystery word.

1. ____ ◯ ____ ____ ____ ____

2. ____ ____ ◯ ____   ____ ____ ____

3. ____ ____ ____ ◯ ____ ____

4. ____ ◯ ____ ____ ____

5. ____ ____ ____ ____ ◯ ____ ____

6. ____ ◯ ____ ____ ____ ____ ____   ____ ____ ____ ____ ____ ____

7. ____ ____ ◯ ____ ____ ____

Mystery word: _____

1. A place that has waterlogged soils and is often covered with shallow water for at least part of the year.

2. A bird bander who needed to capture shorebirds might use one of these.

3. Where an animal lives because it can find food and a place to rest or breed.

4. A type of shorebird habitat with cold winters, short growing seasons, and no trees.

5. How shorebirds get from their breeding grounds to their wintering grounds.

6. The time of the year when shorebirds are in the Arctic.

7. The route birds take during migrations: there are 4 or 5 major ones leading to the Arctic.

Answers: page 35

JOIN THE FLOCK!

Cruise the Super Shorebird Highway at
http://sssp.fws.gov

... and step into the fascinating world of shorebirds.

What's on the Website?

■ You can see video clips of your favorite shorebirds.

■ You can ask biologists questions, learn about shorebirds from other people around the world, and report your own shorebird observations.

■ You can follow as scientists and volunteers track shorebird migration.

■ You can submit your poems, essays, drawings, and pictures to be featured on the Web.

■ You can sign up as a Shorebird Sister School.

ANSWERS

Shorebirds Word Search page 5

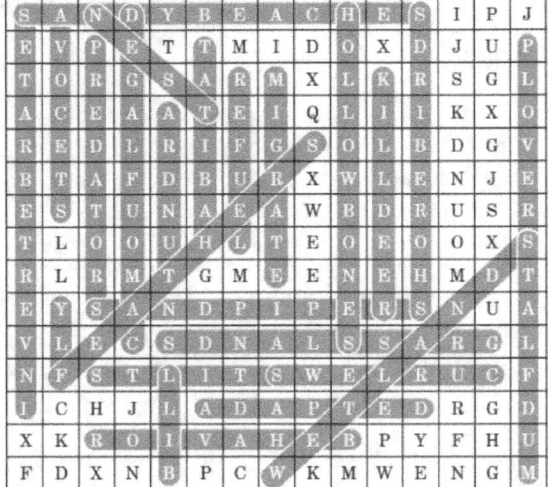

What Can I Eat With This Beak? page 10

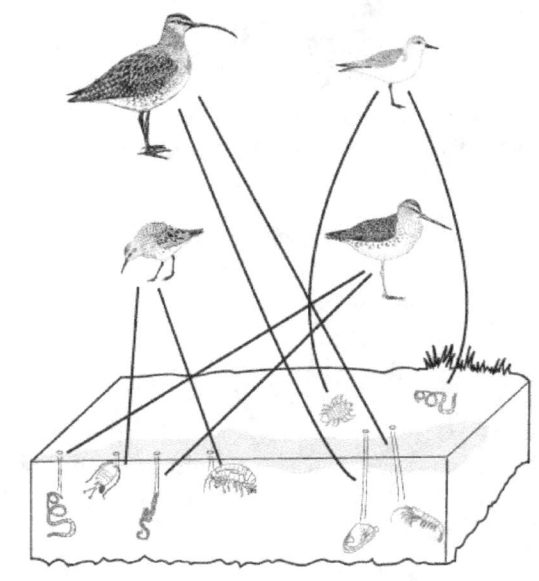

Build a Shorebird, Build Maya page 6

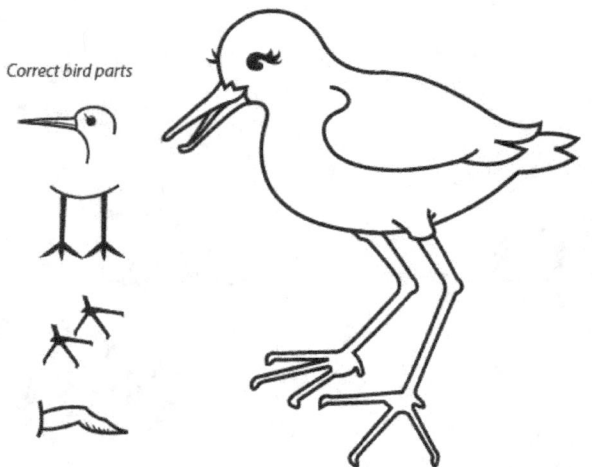

Correct bird parts

Shorebird Migration Word Search page 12

ANSWERS

Shorebird Migration Crossword page 13

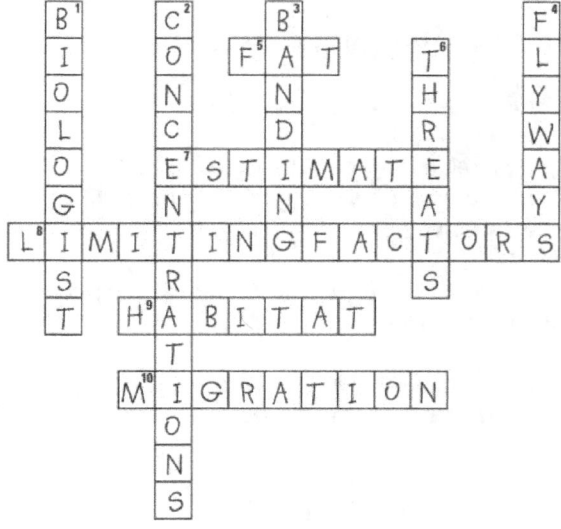

Shorebird Habitat page 17

Super Appetites page 15

80 pounds x 2 = 160
80 + (0.25X) = 160
0.25X = 80
X = 80/0.25
X = 320 hamburgers

or

80 pounds x 2 = 160
160 – 80(present weight) = 80lbs to be gained
1 hamburger =.25 pound
#hamburgers in 80lbs = 80/.25 = 320

Shorebird Breeding Crossword page 18

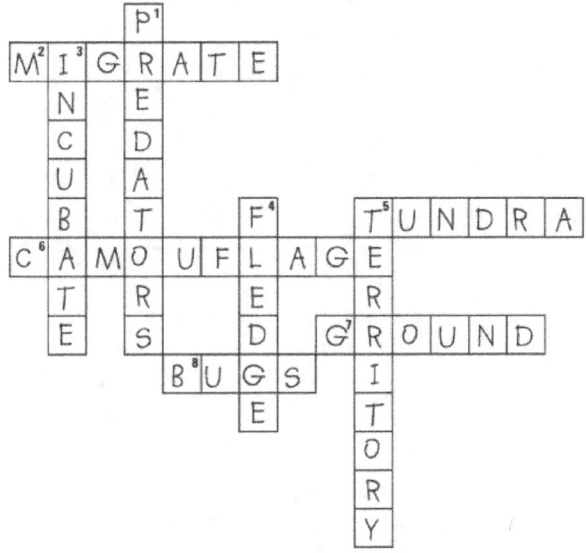

ANSWERS

Wetland Stew Food Chain page 19

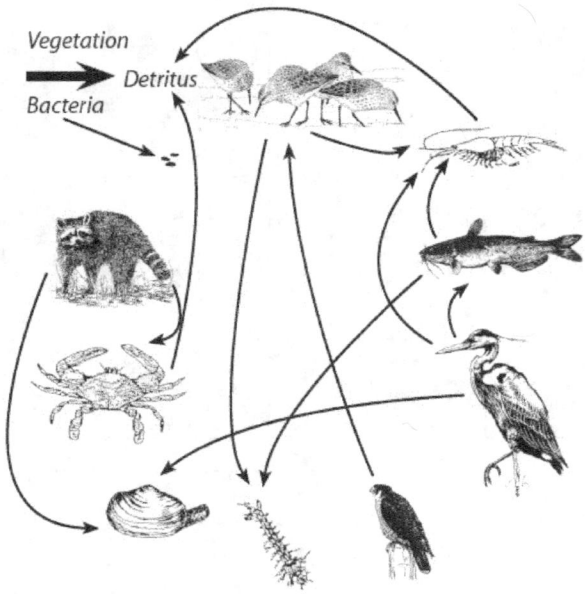

It's a Tough Life For a Super Hero Shorebird page 21

Predators—**fox, cat, gull, raccoon**

Natural events—**hurricane, drought, flood, disease**

Human related— **parking lot, oil spill, trash, polluted water, buildings, filling in wetland, overgrazing**

Which category has the most threats listed under it? **human related**

Which threats can we not control? **natural events, some predators–cats should be indoors**

Can you come up with a solution for one of the human related threats? **pick up trash, prevent oil spills, clean polluted water, keep cats indoors**

Wetland Metaphors page 20

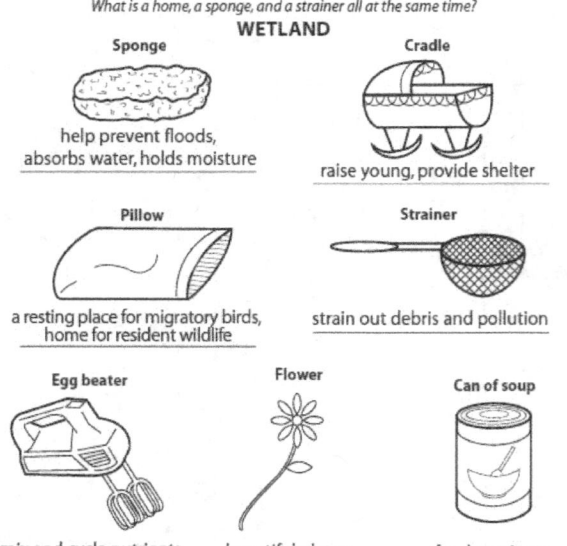

Learning About Shorebirds Is Helping Them! page 29

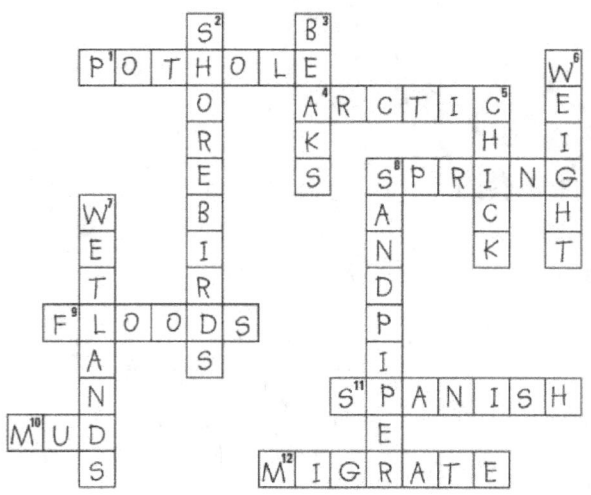

ANSWERS

Shorebird Circle Puzzle page 30

1. WETLAND
2. MIST NET
3. HABITAT
4. TUNDRA
5. MIGRATE
6. BREEDING SEASON
7. FLYWAY

Mystery Word: ESTUARY

U.S. Fish and Wildlife Service
National Conservation Training Center
Shorebird Sister Schools
698 Conservation Way
Shepherdstown, WV
25443

E-mail: sssp@fws.gov
http://sssp.fws.gov

March 2006

http://www.manomet.org/WHSRN

*This Student Activity Guide was
produced by the U.S. Fish and
Wildlife Service's Shorebird Sister
Schools Program.*

*Information, activities, and review
provided by the Western Hemisphere
Shorebird Reserve Network and the
U.S. Fish and Wildlife Service's
National Wildlife Refuges and
Division of Migratory Birds.*

*Thanks to the students and
educators across the United States
who reviewed the guide and provided
valuable comments!*

*The mission of the U.S. Fish and Wildlife Service
is working with others to conserve, protect, and
enhance fish and wildlife and their habitats for
the continuing benefit of the American people.*